THE
VILLAGE
SONNETS:
1959-1962

Also by Michael Lally

THE VILLAGE SONNETS:
1959-1962
Michael Lally

Word Palace Press
P.O. Box 583
San Luis Obispo, CA 93406
wordpalacepress.com
wordpalacepress@aol.com

COVER ARTWORK BY
John Bajet

Cover photo taken in 1964 on Fairchild Air Force Base outside Spokane, Washington after winning a talent contest in the comedy category by drunkenly singing and playing "Gimme That Wine" (and having been asked to remove shades for the shot).

AUTHOR PHOTO BY
Eve Brandstein

The Cornelia Street Cafe in NYC c. 2008

BOOK EDITING AND DESIGN BY
Garrett Stotko and Nadia Ismail

ISBN: 0988804573
ISBN-13:9780988804579

"If you be still and never move, you're gonna dig yourself a well-intentioned rut and think you've found a groove."

—Jon Hendricks

When Nina Simone played THE VILLAGE
GATE I sat on the sidewalk leaning against
the grate above the basement stage, sharing
a bottle of Gallo half-and-half in a brown
paper bag with Destiny and writing poems
to send backstage. She never responded. I
spied James Baldwin once in OBIES. Cliff
said he'd introduce me, but I declined,
having heard he was queer. How would I
handle a pass if he made one? While Baldwin
held court among his admirers, Cliff
told me stories about the people in Harlem
he sold insurance to, as good as Langston
Hughes' *SIMPLE STORIES* only more real.

I took my ex-nun sister to see Nina Simone
who came onstage in a floor-length dress so
tight around her ankles she could take only
tiny steps to get to the piano, a Geisha girl
walking on ice. I heard rumors about her
love life. She was a lesbian, or married to a
cop, or having an affair with the guitarist the
only white man in her band. I championed
the cause of contrast, fixing that sister up
on a date with my drummer friend Sblibby.
It didn't work out. Maureen was an artist
and the coolest white Jersey girl I knew. I
fixed her up with Ralphie, my junkie street
friend. That turned out to be a mistake too.

Princess was a street fixture from the islands.
I never knew which one. I was with her at
OBIES when I first met Cliff, with Mel and
DeWitt. The only empty chairs were at their
table. When we sat down, they started riffing
about how they'd seen Malcolm speak at
the Harlem mosque earlier that week and
he'd asked Have you kicked a white devil
today? And how little white boys were
polluting the race. When I'd had enough
I stood up and said Which one of you
motherfuckers wants to step outside with
me? They laughed and said Sit down,
we're just fooling with you kid. And I did.

Curtis Powell introduced me to my first
Greenwich Village pad. I was seventeen,
already into the Village scene but as a
Jersey interloper digging it from the street.
He took me to the crib of an old white cat
in his thirties and his dark-haired wife in
her twenties, living with a blonde nineteen-
year-old not only pretty but nice. A one-
room studio on Cornelia and Sixth Avenue
with a big bed and little else to sit on and
nowhere else to sleep. It was obvious even
before Curtis hipped me to it, they all slept
together. I thought I preferred black chicks
but if this was beatnik living I wanted some.

Curtis was from South Orange, renowned
for French kissing a white girl in the public
pool in 1957 and smart enough to later earn
a scholarship to college and a PhD. Once he
took me to a rundown little flat on East 2nd
in the building where Ginsberg lived. Bob
Kaufman's crib. He wasn't in, just his dark-
haired Irish-looking wife Eileen and baby
Parker. I read Kaufman's *SECOND APRIL*
for free at Figaro's and smoked my first
joint after a young black dude invited me
to join him for a stroll around the block,
continuing our deep discussion begun inside
reentering with a whole new perspective.

Cliff, Mel and DeWitt lived on West Third near
the strip joints. Mel reminded me of Jackie
Robinson but with a deeper voice and more
eloquent. He spoke German from when they all
met there in the Army after the war. DeWitt was
the Army's first Negro heavyweight champ. Mel
held the yards gained record for college fullbacks.
Cliff, smaller, thinner and lighter skinned, had
a face freckled like mine. He did so well in the
black market he married the first post-war Miss
Berlin and flew her to the states and a house
on Long Island he paid cash for. When she saw
how race played here, she divorced him and
went on to be the blonde in WHITE RAIN ads.

Destiny was one of the gentlest humans
I knew and the first one with no home at all.
One day he jumped out from a doorway to
pull my coat and when I turned around said
Princess is a dyke, she's only using you.
And I said Using me? Someone has found
a use for me? Princess wore men's clothes
that hid a lovely little hourglass figure I
discovered in the bathroom at Mel, Dewitt
and Cliff's fifth floor walkup where we first
made love. It was one of those tiny ones
with only a toilet and water box overhead
you pulled a chain to flush. They took
baths in the kitchen sink, the deep side.

I crashed a Village party with street bros where Red Mitchell was playing with a small combo. When they took a break I stood his bass up and played the melody to *MOANIN'*. Red made it clear he didn't dig strangers playing his ax. I laid it down but drunkenly tripped, putting a tiny crack in it with my pointy-toed boot and was thrown out. For a long time hip Villagers knew me as the little J.D. who kicked a hole in Red Mitchell's bass. At a Brooklyn party Lex Humphries loaned me a rubber when I asked, cause Princess insisted. We went up to the roof, but it was tilted and covered in pebbles that dug into our backs as we almost rolled off.

Met Bob Dylan at THE FAT BLACK PUSSY
CAT before he recorded or I heard him live,
thought he was jive. Passed e. e. cummings in
Washington Square only months before he died.
He looked like an old man, yet bohemian still
in a black beret, a cliché, but not on one from
the generation that created it. Diane di Prima
and Joel Oppenheimer were friendly. Gregory
Corso and LeRoi Jones not. Ginsberg came
across like a pushy hustler at times. Kerouac
drank way too much, like me. We both got 86'd
from THE KETTLE OF FISH. Bob Kaufman,
they said, was part European, African, Asian
and more, which seemed like the future to me.

When Sonny Clark's Trio took a break at THE
WHITE WHALE I sauntered to the piano. Pall
Mall between fingers still able to play, head
drooped toward the keys, a la one of the piano
trinity of my iconic history, Bill Evans, I was
the only white teenage cat with a black soul I
knew. I didn't notice the drummer return till I
heard the shhh shhhh shhhhh of his brushes on
the snare. Now I really felt solid in my groove.
Shit, the cat dug my sound so much he couldn't
resist. Then I grinned as the bass joined in. I
was the featured act now, the cats backing Clark
backing me, making music for all the world to
see, especially my new heart's delight: Bambi.

The song came to an end. The bassist whispered
HONEYSUCKLE ROSE, holding up some fingers
to indicate the key. But it was beyond me, and the
tempo they set was like climbing Mount Everest
in shorts and making it to the top before lunch.
After a few bars I felt a body sit down beside me
on the piano bench. Sonny Clark. He gave me a
pathetic look and swung his hip into mine as
though knocking me out of the way. Which he
was. The band wailed, the audience transfixed as
the white kid took a shaky walk back to his table.
I always wore shades except when in bed so the
tears in my eyes didn't shine in the lights just my
obvious flight from the jazz Olympus in my mind.

The first place I played piano professionally
in Manhattan was on the city's skid row in a
joint with a tourist show called SAMMY'S
BOWERY FOLLIES where ancient weathered
overweight ladies sang like Sophie Tucker,
all brass and sass and volume, and dressed like
19th-century dancehall gals in the Hollywood
Westerns of my boyhood. There were old
men too, vaudeville comics in raggy striped
suits and derbies, and white-haired musicians
playing piano and banjo. My cousin Rosemary
took me and another Irish Catholic girl with
Mary in her name, and her date, certain I'd
pass for eighteen with them in their twenties.

Midway through the show this big bosomed
old lady looked down at our table and asked
who I was, maybe cause I was the youngest
in the club. My cousin said Ricky Nelson.
Invited to the stage I blushed like crazy as the
others insisted I go. Luckily there were no
guitars since I didn't play one. I knew the Fats
Domino song Nelson covered, so I sat down
at the piano to play and sing *I'M WALKIN'*
more like Fats than Ricky I hoped, and felt
gratified by the applause. The manager aware
I wasn't Nelson said he'd pay me to be the
warm-up act for the main show. I did it for a
few months till I discovered progressive jazz.

They called her Bambi cause of her big dark
cartoon-deer eyes that lit up the space around
her. We met in OBIES, the bar on Sixth Ave
across from West Third where I felt most at
home in the world, thanks to a mix of black
and white, old and young, straight and queer,
beat and hipster, junkie and boozer, sophisti-
cated and not, like me who had no idea OBIES
was the name for the off-Broadway theater
awards despite the framed posters of winners
on the walls like *RED EYE OF LOVE*. I thought
Obie was the owner's name. One night there
I spied Bambi at a table with other teenagers
called colored or Negro. Or spade on the street.

After her eyes it was her skin, dark and smooth like coffee without cream, her full lips, nose wide and strong, Indian my spade friends said. Thin as me, a year younger and just graduated from a Catholic girls high school in Atlantic City I learned, after we stop-motion stared at each other before I pulled up a chair. A strange sight to her in my Paul Sargent suit, thin tie and Ray Charles wide-sided shades, a skinny white boy talking bebop Harlem jive. She and her roommate lived on Tompkins Square, the first black chicks there. We made a date. I arrived with Spanish Harry, who wasn't Spanish, and Mamie, the contrast date I'd talked him into.

Already drunk I got aggressive, Bambi later
said, as we sat on her bed. She was scared till
I fell off onto the floor and she couldn't stop
laughing. Next night I came back to see her
again but an old friend from school had shown
up. She was spending the evening with him,
so gave me a rain check. But I never showed,
exposing her I hoped to how much I was hurt,
then felt like a jerk and called to apologize.
She said she waited for hours. Next time we
met at OBIES where we learned we had even
more in common. Like our fathers: self-made,
grammar-school dropouts with high-school
educated wives. Soon we were a Village item.

I was known among friends and family for
falling in love at the drop of an eyelash. But
this time was different. Even Mel, Cliff and
DeWitt got the intensity of it. We spent every
second we could with each other, getting close
to making love completely then backing off
to save her virginity for the night of our wedding we needed our parents permission for,
too young to marry in Jersey or New York.
In states where we weren't, our so-called
races made it against the law. My father said
Men and women are different, so you start
with one strike against you. If the woman's
not Irish, that's two. Not Catholic, you're out.

When my music-man brother Buddy wanted
to marry my Italian sister-in-law, there were
whispered admonitions behind closed doors
about what would be in store for them and
their kids. That sense of forbidden fruit fueled
my boyhood crush on her dark Italian beauty.
My father couldn't argue that we had three
strikes against us: Bambi was Catholic. But
he argued anyway, that our kids would have
it too hard. Out of his hearing, ma said in
tears I don't care who you marry if you love
each other but I have to back your father,
he's my husband. Bambi's father hated
white people for what they'd done to him.

The night we gave up any hope of marrying before she turned twenty-one, three long years away, I decided Fuck them all. Fuck our families fuck society fuck the stupid racial laws. Then we finally made love all the way as she whispered I'm sorry. I asked What for? That I couldn't wait till we were married. But I swore before God we were husband and wife. She always said I was her first lover. Though I had others, like Princess and Dolores, I felt she was my first too. Later lying in each other's arms she said I love you, in a way so surrendered, so deeply sincere, so much an echo of the feelings in my heart toward her, I knew it was true.

Bambi's roommate didn't dig me so we
hung at Mel, Cliff and Dewitt's talking and
making love when they were out. They gave
us a key. This was before Cliff got his own
place after walking in on Mel having sex
with Cliff's lady, the Harlem beauty Theresa.
Cliff and Mel were back being friends
before long, but Theresa was gone. Cliff's
new pad on Thompson had two bedrooms.
He rented one to Bull, a married man who
used it with just a mattress on the floor for
his rendezvous. Bambi and I used it too.
There were no examples of happy and
accepted mixed-race marriages we knew.

Mixed couples were rare, and outside The Village found only in black neighborhoods, where it was always black men with white women. My Jersey friends Teddy and Lynn seemed truly happy, but Lyn worked in an office in Newark where her coworkers were not even aware she was married to a Negro. Her Italian relatives were. And her mother lived with them. My brother-in-law Joe the cop and me were working on the rectory roof one day when Teddy rode by on his Harley. Joe couldn't stop talking about The flying jig on a motorcycle. Teddy treated Joe as he did everyone, with kind acceptance.

White people in our parish were upset when
Teddy and Lynn got married in our church,
the first mixed-race wedding there. Except
for parties at their East Orange pad they didn't
socialize much. Just going to the store, people
stared or pointed or made nasty remarks. There
were no movies or books with happy stories
of mixed-race romance, let alone marriage.
Kerouac's short novel about his affair with a
black lady, *THE SUBTERRANEANS*, didn't
end happily. In the movie version she's played
by Leslie Caron. The closest Hollywood
would come to a mixed-race romance was to
turn the black chick into a white French one.

THE NEW YORK TIMES ran an article on
teens who copied the Beat or hip style but
came from Jersey or Long Island to The
Village on weekends. DOWNSTAIRS AT
THE DUPLEX had a piano I played when
no one else did. Like the day someone said
There's a reporter at MARIES CRISIS CAFÉ
looking for teenagers who aren't Village
natives. We knew it was us in the story,
the only mixed teenage couple then. The
original Marie was a Gypsy, but now was
a big black lady who played piano and sang.
Her most popular song's refrain was *No-
body cans cans like the garbage man can.*

Ted Joans was known as a Beat poet who ex-
ploited the tourist trade, a reputedly hip spade
usually wearing a black beret when I saw him.
In a photo in *THE BEAT SCENE* he sat on the
grass in Washington Square Park with a white
woman and four mixed kids and talked about
Loving every swinging soul. But he gave Bambi
a hard time cause I was white. She was so darkly
beautiful, older black men wanted to protect her
or make her their own. Everyone noticed her
lovely face and lithe figure as she danced bare
foot on the grass in the park in flowery summer
dresses, a darker apparition and prediction of
what hippies would be like several years later.

Big Brown was a giant of a man, six-
feet-a-lot, with a fierce expression on
his dark face and a way of intimidating
everyone. One day in OBIES he told
Bambi she was wasting her foxy female
self on a skinny little nothing of a sheet,
a gray, a Mister Charlie, just as Cliff
walked in. Before I jumped salty, Cliff
said in his laconic way that if Brown dug
being black so much how come his hair
was gassed? A withering comment about
Brown's conk, a wavy almost Marcel
curl. Brown seemed to cringe, then huffed
and puffed some before disappearing.

In Harlem after visiting a musician friend
on Sugar Hill, me and Bambi following
arcane directions to the subway suddenly
were surrounded by a gang of twenty
or more younger black boys wanting to
know what I was doing with her on their
streets. I said I'm walking with the woman
I love. One of the young dudes who wasn't
the hostile leader, but obviously had influence, said Aw leave the cat alone. And
they did. More often it was whites giving
us trouble outside the Village. Cursing us
or making threats, or even spitting, like a
sailor did at me in Times Square daylight.

The first time we slept with other street kids
in the empty fountain in Washington Square
we woke at dawn and went to the small
water fountain for a drink. I splashed some
on Bambi in fun, but she got all tight-jawed.
When she calmed down, she explained if
her hair, already misshapen from sleeping
on concrete, got wet, it would tighten up
and look even worse. I made sure I never
did that to any black woman again. I wrote
a story about it, adding it to some of the
ones I sent to magazines every week to
always keep some in the mail no matter how
many came back. Like that one kept doing.

When the bulls drove through the Washington
Square arch, like buses did to turn around till
they made Fifth Avenue one way, they'd roust
street kids sleeping in the fountain when dry.
I'd act all innocent and square when they asked
for my I.D. and saw I was from Jersey. Like
I was just a teenage tourist looking for Greenwich Village kicks and got caught up with
the runaways, the teenage vipers and juvenile
delinquents, as I was called across the Hudson
and by some Villagers who knew me. Others
would say I was a little Jersey jitterbug or teenage version of what Norman Mailer wrote his
famous essay about: *THE WHITE NEGRO.*

Cal was Mel's twin but opposite. A high school drop out with a wife and four kids in Pennsylvania, he talked fast with a distinct private accent difficult to understand. Mel enunciated every word like a 19th-century orator. Cal was thinner and darker, with a nose so long and sharply hooked he could pass in profile for an ancient Egyptian. He'd been a paratrooper at fifteen, lying about his age, in post-war Japan then Korea. Mel wore impeccable suits. Cal funky sweatshirts and jeans. Once, walking up the Bowery, on that island where it turns into Third Ave, Cal shouted out to the rainy night: New York, you don't owe me a thing!

Sblibby named himself after the black street
term for what Southern racists called niggery,
pushing it in everyone's face. Ebony toned,
my height and weight, but more sinewy and
tight and a few years older, like me he wore
shades indoors and out every waking hour.
I never knew his real name. We met one
rainy afternoon when we were the only ones
at the bar in OBIES. Me at one end, him at
the other with drum sticks and a rubber
practice pad. Yaya let him play along with
the box since we were the only ones there.
When Eric Dolphy blew a phrase that made
us both laugh, we recognized each other.

Sblibby came into OBIES one afternoon with
a short dark man wearing thick eyeglasses
on his intense angry face. It was Cecil Taylor,
the piano-playing composer innovator changing
jazz. When I extended my hand to slip him
some skin he curled his lip in distaste. Sblib
didn't notice as he raved about me, suggesting
Taylor come to THE WHITE WHALE where
I could display my chops. Surprisingly he did.
There I started in on my version of Ahmad
Jamal's take on *SURREY WITH THE FRINGE
ON TOP*, only even more up-tempo so even
more difficult. But after only a few bars Taylor
got up and walked out without saying a word.

In the West Fourth Street station I ran into
Angela and told her about Bambi. She got
upset and wrote me later *You were meant
to marry me, if you marry a colored girl
neither race will accept your kids.* Bambi
quit her job under the influence of Villagers
who promoted free love and life, strangers
to me. Like Chico, light-brown-skinned with
thick black hair, usually taken for a Puerto
Rican. He was skinny like Bambi and me,
but quieter than I could be. She wanted us
to hang together. But he had neither a job
nor home so was free to roam the Village
streets with her while I was busy working.

When Bambi said Chico was so broke he ate dog
food out of a can cause it was cheaper than Spam,
I ordered her not to see him anymore. She laughed
and went on doing what she wanted. I wanted a
darker version of Dostoevsky's Anna, not a free
spirit. I got so jealous, uptight and tired of her new
friends and life, when Chico came into OBIES
looking for her, I shoved him against a wall and
spit: I'll rip your lungs out through your throat if
you hurt her. Then drunkenly decided to join the
Army to show them both. My crippled grandma
who lived with us since Grandpa Dempsey died
always accused me of cutting off my nose to spite
my face. I never understood what she meant by it.

In my usual jazzman's outfit, shades and all,
I went to enlist at the Orange Post Office near
Orange Memorial Hospital where I was born.
An Air Force recruiter leaning against a wall
said What's happenin' man? A hip greeting for
any white man then, let alone one in uniform.
He stuck out his hand, and when I reflexively
did too, slapped mine, an even rarer thing for
a gray dude to do. He said the Army's no place
for a hip cat like you, but the Air Force is full
of hip mixed couples. He swore once they saw
me in uniform, Bambi would come running,
our fathers would give in, and I'd be playing
piano in an officer's club in The Big Apple.

I signed up for the four-year enlistment. Told
to report to New York the next day I made my
Jersey goodbyes, then met Mel at DOWN-
STAIRS AT THE DUPLEX. Arriving first I
went to the unoccupied piano. After I played
a few tunes the owner said his piano player
split and offered me the job at a hundred a
month. Cliff paid thirty for his two bedroom
pad. I could support the city life I'd always
fantasized. But too late. When Mel arrived I
told him. He laughed, seeing the humor in it.
I didn't. At OBIES, Cal, Cliff and DeWitt sent
me off with many toasts, Cliff calling me Me-
shell, as he always did, adding Bon voyage.

For unexplained reasons we were given three
more days of freedom. I spent it getting drunk
and high with street friends like Andre, a tall
dark junkie who knew where to crash. But the
last night I ended up alone in a bar unable to
stand. When they 86'd me, this square looking
Irish chick helped me walk to her crib on East
11th where to my surprise she lived with Pauline
a light-skinned mixed teen from Long Island
City who ran away at fifteen to arrive in the
Village pregnant. Before she began showing,
she had a body men fought over. But she was
too tough for me. Maybe she had to be. She
hooked to get by. Turned out Irish did too.

Stumbling in, we woke Pauline up. She threw
a clock at us but gave me one twin bed to sleep
in and they took the other. I woke at dawn to
stare at these two women an arm's length away,
Pauline on the outside, Irish against the wall.
The covers had slid down and one of Pauline's
legs dangled off the side, her slip up past her
thighs so everything was showing. I had my
horrible hangover, able to focus on nothing but
Pauline's everything, feeling oppressed by it,
as though it was all I was running from. The
power that morsel of female flesh had over me.
The Irish Catholic pain and shame and guilt it
represented. I split without saying goodbye.

About the Author

Michael Lally was born in Orange, New Jersey in 1942 and published his first poem at age 18. After serving four years in the military, he used the GI Bill to attend the University of Iowa Writers Workshop, and as a result of his political activism there was nominated by The Peace and Freedom Party to run for sheriff of Johnson County, Iowa, in 1968.

Since then, Lally has fought for racial justice and the rights of women and minorities, including the LGBT community, while working as a musician, editor, college teacher, book critic (for *The Washington Post* and The *Village Voice*), night guard, chauffeur, actor, screenwriter and script doctor.

Lally is the author of twenty-eight books of poetry and is often associated with the New York School of Poetry. He counts among his early influences the poets Frank O'Hara, William Carlos Williams, Bob Kaufman, and Diane di Prima, the jazz singer and lyricist Jon Hendricks, as well as the writer William Saroyan.

He is the recipient of numerous awards including two National Endowment for the Arts grants and the American Book Award in 2000 for *It's Not Nostalgia*. He currently lives in New Jersey and writes the blog *Lally's Alley*.

OTHER BOOKS FROM WORD PALACE PRESS

HOW STRANGE IT IS TO BE ANYTHING AT ALL
Joe Riley

IMAGINERY BURDEN
Michael Hannon

A POEM OF MIRACLES
Jerome Rothenberg

CELTIC LIGHT
Lee Perron

BORDER SONGS
Sam Hamill

UNDER SUCH BRILLIANCE
Kevin Patrick Sullivan

BEAUTY LIKE A ROPE
Leslie St. John

WAYFARING STRANGER
Richard Tillinghast

LIFE
Jack Foley

WHO ON EARTH
Michael Hannon

INSTRUCTIONS FOR THE LIVING
Mariko Nagai

TILTING POINT
Peter Dale Scott

FORTHCOMING TITLES

WOMEN UNDER THE INFLUENCE
Michael C. Ford

SISTER MADELINE
Joe Riley